Words of Love
A Collection of Quotes
About Love

Created By

Ian Wilson

ISBN: 9781461118718

Printed in U.S.A

www.wordsoflove.ca

Introduction

Very often in life we come across words
of love that touch our hearts.
This happened to me very often,
so, I started keeping a collection of quotes
that I came across.
Now I have decided to share my collection
with you.
Some of them will make us think about our
present partner.
Others might bring thoughts of love desired
or lost.
Love comes from the heart.
Love is something that we all desire.
It brings peace into our souls.
It gives us a zest for life, which material
possessions cannot do.
We can feel empty without love.
I hope that you will enjoy my collection and
that the love in your heart will continue to
grow.

Come live in my heart and pay no rent.

Samuel Lover

Should I smile because we are friends?
Or cry because we will never be anything
more?

Think to thank. In these three words is the
finest capsule course for a happy marriage.
A formula for enduring friendship and a
pattern for personal happiness.

Thomas S. Monson

Today I caught myself smiling then I realized
that I was thinking about you.

I was finally getting over you and believing that I didn't need you.
I finally accepted the fact that you had another girl.
Then you smiled at me and ruined it all.

The worst feeling you will ever have is sitting next to the person who means the world to you, knowing that you mean nothing to them.

I am jealous of the people that you hugged today because for a moment they held my world.

It takes a minute to have a crush on someone, an hour to like someone and a day to love someone but it takes a lifetime to forget someone.

Her eyes, her lips, her cheeks, her shape,
her features seem to be drawn by love's
own hand, by love himself in love.

There are many things in life that will catch
your eyes but only a few will catch your
heart, pursue those.

There is nothing more beautiful than a person
whose heart has been broken but still believes
in love.

Sticks and stones are hard on
Bones aimed with angry art.
Words can sting like anything
But silence breaks the heart.

People will forget what you said.
People will forget what you did.
But people will never forget the
way you made them feel.

If someone makes you miserable more than
they make you happy, it doesn't matter how
much you love them, you need to let them go.

It is a cold sheet that only one person sleeps
under.

Loving someone who doesn't love you back
is like hugging a cactus.
The tighter you hold on, the more it hurts.

Love is an act of endless forgiveness, a tender
look which becomes a habit.

A woman's happiness is not in the glory and lordship of a man. Neither is it in his generosity or clemency; it is in a love that binds her spirit to his spirit, pouring out her love into his heart and making them a single member in the body of Life and one word on the lips of God.

Seduce my mind and you can have my body. Find my soul and I am yours forever.

Love is shown in your deeds not only in your words.

Fr. Jerome Cummings

Better a dish of vegetables if love goes with it, than a fat ox eaten in hatred.

Prov. 15:17

Love and fidelity have come together;
justice and peace join hands.

Ps. 85:10

The hottest love has the coldest end.

Socrates

I love you not because of whom you are but
because of who I am when I am with you.

There is no force in this world that can rob
me of my happiness, for it springs from the
embrace of two souls held together by
understanding and sheltered by love.

I want to be his favorite hello and his hardest goodbye.

Those whom Love has not chosen as followers do not hear when Love calls.

The Broken Wings

In a true relationship, your partner is also your best friend.

Good marriages are made in heaven.

He's more myself than I am.
Whatever our souls are made of,
his and mine are the same.

Emily Bronte

The spaces between your fingers were created so that another's could fill them.

If you love someone tell them, because hearts are often broken by words left unspoken.

Every time a lady smiles at me
or says, "Hello" I get my fix.
Today I had an overdose.

If I could choose between breathing and loving you, I would use my last breath to say, "I love you."

If the essence of my being has caused a smile to have appeared upon your face or a touch of joy within your heart.
Then in living I have made my mark.

It's hard when someone special ignores you.
It's harder pretending that you just don't care.

What do you do when the only one that can
stop you from crying is the person who made
you start crying?

Sometimes you need to run away, just to
see who will come after you.

Cute is good but cute only lasts for so long,
then it's, "who are you as a person?
That's the advice I would give to women.
Don't look at the bank book or the title.
Look at the heart. Look at the soul.
Look at how the guy treats his mother and
what he says about women.
Look at how he acts with children and more
important, how he treats you."

Michelle Obama

9

I wish that I had the guts to walk away from what we have.
I can't because I know that you won't come after me.
That is what hurts me the most.

When I first saw you, I was afraid to talk to you.
When I first talked to you I was afraid to like you.
When I first liked you, I was afraid to love you.
Now that I love you, I am afraid to lose you.

One day you're going to look back and say, "Damn that girl really did love me."

To be capable of a steady friendship and lasting love is proof of a good heart and a strong mind.

Looking back, I have this to regret, that
too often when I loved I did not say so.

To love is to admire with the heart.
To admire is to love with the mind.

Love doesn't make the world go around.
Love is what makes the ride worthwhile.

Love is a friend, a fire a heaven a hell;
where pleasure, pain and sad repentance
dwell.

Richard Bernfield

Love cures people both the ones who give it
and the ones who receive it.

Dr. Karl Menninger

It hurts to let go but sometimes it hurts more
to hold on.

Whether it's a friendship or
relationship, all bonds are built on trust.
Without it you have nothing.

Destiny determines who comes into our lives
but it's the heart that decides who stays
inside.

The decision to kiss for the first time is the most crucial in any love story.
It changes the relationship of the two people more strongly than even the final surrender, because this kiss already has within it that surrender.

Emil Ludwig

You promised that you would never leave. Where are you now?

Love is saying, "I feel differently instead of, "your wrong."

The excess of love will soon pass but its inefficiency torments us forever.

Find a heart that will love you at your worst and arms that will hold you at your weakest.

Distance doesn't matter if two hearts are loyal to each other.

There are a million things in the world I want but all I need is you.

Love is the triumph of imagination over intelligence.

Why love if losing hurts so much?
We love to know that we are not alone.

Clive Staples Lewis

Love makes your soul crawl out from its
hiding place.

After I fell in love with you, I fell in love with
my life.

How shall my heart be unsealed unless it is
broken?

To love and be loved is to feel the sun from both sides.

How bold one gets when one is sure of being loved.

Sigmund Freud

Kindness in women not their beauteous looks shall win my love.

William Shakespeare

To love yourself is the beginning of a lifelong romance.

We all need unconditional love and acceptance.

Never frown because you never know who might be falling in love with your smile.

If there ever comes a day when we can't be together, keep me in your heart.
I'll stay forever.

A capable wife is her husband's crown.

I get the best feeling in the world when you say, "hi" or even smile at me because I know that even if it was just for a second, that I have crossed your mind.

You are what you attract yourself to.

So dear I love him, that with him all death
I could endure. Without him live no life.

Romeo and Juliet, William Shakespeare

Love and a cough cannot be hidden.

George Herbert

A broken-hearted lady said, "He is my
livelihood, my best friend, he completes me."

Ever has it been that love knows not its own depth until the hour of separation.

An intelligent wife is a gift from the Lord.

Prov. 19:13

Love is a smoke made with the fume of sighs.

William Shakespeare

You know you're in love when you don't want to fall to sleep because reality is finally better than your dreams.

Dr. Seuss

A heart that loves is always young.

Greek Proverb

Love is patient love is kind and envies no one.
Love is never boastful, nor conceited, nor
rude; never selfish, not quick to take offense.

The anger of love renews the strength of love.

When I met you I found life.
If I lose you I cannot live.

Equality is the firmest bond of love.

Reproof on her lips but a smile in her eyes.

Absence in love is like water upon fire.
A little quickens but much extinguishes.

Find that guy that will pick up every piece of
your shattered heart and put it back together.
Keeping one piece for himself, replacing it
with a piece of his.

The times we were happy together are worth
the times I cry alone.

Love turns a blind eye to every fault.

They say time heals all but without you
by my side, time stands still.

Love me and the world is mine.

Lope De Vega

The love game is never called off because of
darkness.

Tom Mason

Pain of love be sweeter far, than all other
pleasures are.

Torn between two whom would you choose, the one that you love or the one that loves you?

We are never so defenseless against suffering as when we love.

Sigmund Freud

The course of true love never did run smooth.

Love is an irresistible desire to be irresistibly desired.

Love is an act of acceptance regardless of our imperfections.

No road is too long with good company.

Turkish Proverb

Lots of people will ride with you in the limo
but what you want is someone who will take
the bus with you when the limo breaks down.

Oprah Winfrey

I don't wish to be everything to everyone
but I would like to be something to someone.

Love is much like a wild rose, beautiful and
calm but willing to draw blood in its defense.

When death to either shall come,
I pray it be first to me.

Robert Bridges

Some people think that to be strong is to
never feel pain.
In reality the strongest people are the ones
who feel it, understand it and accept it.

Is life worth living without somebody to love
and to be loved in return?

Zen Joy Pym

Love is a language spoken by everyone but
understood only by the heart.

Delicacy is to love what grace is to beauty.

French Proverb

Your task is not to seek for love but merely to seek and find all the barriers within yourself that you have built against it.

Love me without fear.
Trust me without questioning.
Need me without demanding.
Want me without restrictions.
Accept me without change.
Desire me without inhibitions.
If only it were that way, if only.

Pleasure of love lasts but a moment.
Pain of love lasts a life time.

Bette Davis.

We waste time looking for the perfect lover,
instead of creating the perfect love.

When silence speaks for Love she has much
to say.

Richard Garnett

The standard of success in life isn't the things
you have.
It isn't the money, it is the amount of joy you
feel.

In your life you meet people, some you never
think about again.
Some you wonder what happened to them.
There are some that you wonder if they ever
think about you.
Then there are some you wish you never had
to think about again, but you do.

There is one sad truth in life I've found
while journeying east and west.
The only folks we really wound,
Are those we love the best.
We flatter those we scarcely know,
We please the fleeting guest.
Then deal full many thoughtless blows,
to those whom love us best.

Consider how hard it is to change yourself
and you will understand what little chance
you have in trying to change others.

We choose those we like.
With those we love, we have no say in the
matter.

Are we not like two volumes of one book?

Marceline Desbordes Valmor

Someone to tell it to is one of the fundamental needs of human beings.

Miles Franklin

Promises mean everything but after they are broken, promises mean nothing.

Let us be grateful to people who make us happy.
They are the charming gardeners who make our souls blossom.

To know when to go away and when to come closer is the key to any lasting relationship.

Falling in love is awfully simple but falling out of love is simply awful.

We are each a planet orbiting somebody's sun, unconscious of a lonely moon orbiting our planet.

Every time I see him all cool, calm and collected, I lose my breath.
My heart starts pounding and I'm painfully aware that I'm not over him and that he is over me.

Love is the condition in which the happiness of another person is essential to your own.

Love is a wildly misunderstood although a
highly desirable malfunction of the heart.
It weakens the brain, causes eyes to sparkle,
cheeks to glow, blood to pressure and the lips
to pucker.

Love either finds equality or makes it.

Do not get mad when a girl cares too much.
Worry when she starts not to care anymore.

You are the air that I breathe.
I love you beyond the depths of my soul.

Love comforts like sunshine after rain.

The hardest thing to do is waking up without you.

Men are easy to find but love is nowhere to be found.

Someone has stolen my heart and you are the highest on my list of suspects.

What happens when he's your prince charming but you're not his Cinderella?

In the enriching of marriage, the big things
are the little things.
It is a constant appreciation for each other
and a thoughtful demonstration of gratitude.
It is the encouraging and helping each other
to grow.
Marriage is a joint quest for the good, the
beautiful and the divine.

James E. Faust

Love is taking two hearts and blending them
into one.

Thou art my life, my love, my heart.

If today I die, I will be at peace because
I have known my soul mate and have
understood the true meaning of love.

It's not a lack of love but a lack of friendship that makes unhappy marriages.

Don't say, "You miss me" when it's your fault I'm gone.

If you judge people, you have no time to love them.

Mother Teresa

Love looks not with the eyes but with the mind.

William Shakespeare

Love never dies a natural death.
It dies because we don't know how to
replenish its source.
It dies of blindness, errors and betrayals.
It dies of illness and wounds, it dies of
weariness, of withering, of tarnishing.

Anais Nin

Some wounds never truly heal and bleed
again at the slightest word.

Cry as I may, these tears won't wash away.

A moment in my arms forever in my heart.

Love is needing someone.
Love is putting up with someone's bad
qualities because some how they complete
you.

If you have love in your life, it can make up
for a great many things you lack.
If you don't have it, no matter what you do
have in your life, it is not enough.

The greater the love the greater the tragedy
when it's over.

For it was not into my ear you whispered
but into my heart.
It was not my lips you kissed but my soul.

Judy Garland

Every time you smile at someone,
it is an action of love, a gift to that person,
a beautiful thing.

When people can walk away from you let them walk.
Your destiny is never tied to anybody who has left.

True love is not so much a matter of romance as it is a matter of anxious concern for the well-being of one's partner.

Gordon B Hinckley

Suppressing love is but opposing the natural dictates of the heart.

The hunger for love is much more difficult to remove than the hunger for bread.

Mother Teresa

Morning without you is a dwindled dawn.

The greater a man's soul, the deeper he loves.

Leonardo DaVinci

I heard what you said; I am not the silly
romantic you think. I don't want the heavens
or the shooting stars. I don't want gemstones
or gold. I have those things already.
I want a steady hand and a kind soul.
I want to fall asleep and wake knowing my
heart is safe. I want to love and be loved.

Shana Abe

You can't buy love because when it's real it's
priceless.

You must learn to let go and move on,
instead of carrying the pain in you.
You don't have the right to cause pain to
yourself.

The eyes shout what the lips fear to say.

When I saw you, I fell in love and you smiled
because you knew.

William Shakespeare

If he loved you with all the power of his soul
for a whole lifetime, he couldn't love you as
much as I do in a single day.

Give me chastity but not yet.

St. Augustine

If a man wants you, nothing can keep him
away.
If he doesn't want you, nothing can make
him stay.

A man can be so changed by love as to be
unrecognizable as the same person.

It's hard to wait around for something
you know might never happen.
It's even harder to give up when it's
everything you want.

A love took an early root and had an early doom.

Love understands love, it needs no talk.

I want a girl just like the girl that married dear old dad.

The voice of love seemed to call me, but it was a wrong number.

How do I love thee? Let me count the ways.

Elizabeth Barrett Brown

There is no greater glory than love or any
greater punishment than jealousy.

It warms me, it charms me, to mention
her name.
It heats me it beats me and sets me on flame.

The last time I saw you, I said it hurt too
much to love you but I was wrong about that.
The truth is, it hurts too much not to love you.

I love thee, I love thee and it's all that I can
say.
It is my vision in the night, my dreaming in
the day.

It is better to be lonely on your own than
to be lonely with someone else.

If I had a flower for every time I thought of
you, I could walk through my garden forever.

Alfred Tennyson

Love embraces a woman's whole life,
it is her prison and her kingdom of heaven.

Chamisso

And then he gave me a smile that was so
genuinely sweet, with just the right touch
of shyness, an unexpected warmth rushed
through me.

Suzanne

The sweet love that captured me, transformed
into bitter despair.

The man I loved fell out of love with me.
My heart was broken, my spirit shattered.

A lady's imagination is very rapid;
it jumps from admiration to love,
from love to matrimony in a moment.

Jane Austen

If love is the answer, could you rephrase
the question?

So sweet love seemed that April morn,
When first we kissed beside the thorn.
So strangely sweet, it was not strange,
We thought that love could never change.

Never love anyone who treats you like your
ordinary.

Oscar Wilde

Being deeply loved by someone gives you
strength, while loving someone deeply
gives you courage.

Lao Tzu

Love is like the wind; you can't see it but you can feel it.

Nicholas Sparks

Have you ever been in love? Horrible isn't it?
It makes you so vulnerable.
It opens your chest, it opens up your heart and it means that someone can get inside you and mess you up.

Love all, trust a few, do wrong to none.

You don't love someone because they're perfect; you love them in spite of the fact that they're not.

The more I know of the world, the more I am convinced that I shall never see a man whom I can really love. I require so much.

Jane Austen

And in the end, the love you take is equal to the love you make.

Recipe for Love

Ingredients

1 cup of romance
1 pinch of humour
2 spoonful's of joy
1lb of Compatibility
3 Tb of trust
1 cup of respect
½ lbs. of sharing
1 zest of tenderness
¾ cup of patience

My heart skips a beat every time I see you but my heart completely stopped when I saw you with her.

When you truly love someone, you give everything you can and never expect a return.

The surest way to hit a woman's heart is to take aim kneeling.

Sometimes the strongest people are the ones who love beyond all faults, cry behind closed doors and fight battles that nobody knows about.

True love doesn't have a happy ending
because true love never ends.

One of the hardest things in life is watching
the one you adore love someone else.

Give me a thousand kisses and yet more,
Then repeat those that have gone before.

Look not for beauty or the color of skin,
But look for the heart that is loyal within.
For beauty will fade and skin will grow old
But a heart that is loyal will never grow cold.

One day someone is going to hug you so tight
that all of your broken pieces will stick back
together.

Real love is not based on romance, candle
light dinners and walks along the beach.
It is based on respect, compromise,
care and trust.

Everybody knows how to love but few people
know how to stay in love with one person
forever.

One smile can start a friendship.
One word can end a fight.
One look can save a relationship.
One person can change your life.

The truth hurts but silence kills.

Better an old man's darling than a young
man's slave.

When a woman is loved truly, unconditionally
and eternally, she doesn't care what car her
man drives or what he wears.
She is just content with the ways she is loved
and she will do anything to be with the man
who loves her soul and never give up on him.

Aarti Khurana

Charm is a delusion and beauty fleeting.
It is the God-fearing woman who is honored.

Prov. 31:30

Everyone who is in your life is meant to be
a part of that journey but not all of them are
meant to stay.

A person who truly loves you is someone who sees pain in your eyes, while everyone else still believes in the smile on your face.

When she kissed him he melted like a lump of milk chocolate.

A woman who doesn't ask for anything deserves everything.

No matter how old you both get, never stop holding hands, never stop dancing and never stop saying, "I love you."

A good boyfriend will never want to change anything about you except your last name.

She straightens her hair, puts on her eyeliner, glosses her lips and takes one last look in the mirror, all for the boy who will never care.

A true man does more than promise,
he commits.

No person has the right to condemn you on how you repair your heart or how long you choose to grieve, because no one knows how much you're hurting.
Recovering takes time and everyone heals at his or her own pace.

Relationships last longer when nobody knows your business.

The best kind of relationship in the world, is the one in which a "sorry" and a "smile" can make everything go back to normal again.

My definition of love is you.

Everyone says that love hurts but that's not true. Loneliness hurts, losing someone hurts. Everyone confuses these things with love. Love is the only thing in this world that covers up all the pain and makes us feel wonderful again.

Equality is no rule in love's grammar.

Beaumont and Fletcher

Although you can't be with me, we're truly
not apart.
Until the final breath I take, you'll be living
in my heart.

Love is the most beautiful thing to have,
hardest thing to earn and most painful
thing to lose.

The greatest thing a man can do to a woman
is to lead her closer to God than to himself.

Tears are words from the heart that can't
be spoken.

Everyone comes with baggage.
Find someone who loves you enough
to help you unpack.

You'll know when a relationship is right
for you.
It will enhance your life, not complicate
your life.

Woman came from man's rib.
Not from his feet to be walked on.
Not from his head to be superior.
But from his side to be equal, under his arm to
be protected and close to his heart to be loved.

Hurt me with the truth but never comfort
me with a lie.

Heaven has no rage like love to hatred turned.
Nor Hell a fury like a woman scorned.

My heart is entwined around yours forever
and ever.

Love alone is capable of uniting living beings
in such a way as to complete and fulfill them.
It takes them and joins them to what is
deepest within themselves.

Sometimes I may hate you, but I'll always
love you.

No one in this world is pure and perfect.
If you avoid people for their mistakes,
you will always be alone in this world.

If I could give you one thing in life,
I would give you the ability to see yourself
through my eyes.
Only then would you realize how special you
are to me.

My heart longs for you, my soul dies for you.
My eyes cry for you; my empty arms reach
out for you.

One day someone will walk into your life
and make you see why it never worked out
with anyone else.

Loved you yesterday, love you still.
Always have, always will.

A crush is love with an expiry date.

Be mindful of what you throw away.
Be careful of what you push away.
Think hard before you walk away.

At times our own light goes out and is
rekindled by a spark from another person.
Each one of us has cause to think deep
gratitude of those who have lit the flame
within.

The Art of Marriage

A good marriage must be created.
In marriage, the little things are the big things
It's never being too old to hold hands.
It's remembering to say, "I love you" at the
end of each day. It is never going to bed
angry.
It is speaking words of appreciation and
demonstrating gratitude in thoughtful ways.
It is having the capacity to forgive and forget.
It is giving each other a safe place in which to
grow. It is not only marrying the right person,
it is being the right partner.

William Peterson

We are shaped and fashioned by what we
love.

When you plant a seed of love, it is you
that blossoms.

In loving his wife, a man loves himself.

Love is a partnership of two people who
bring out the very best in each other.
They know that even though they are
wonderful individuals, they are even better
together.

Some men focus more on how to get a
woman but once they have her, lose focus
on how to keep her.

Weeping may endure for a night but joy
comes in the morning.

Psalms 30:5

Follow love and it will flee, flee love
and it will follow thee.

Spread love everywhere you go.
Let no one ever come to you without
leaving happier.

Mother Teresa

A broken trust can be described as melted
chocolate. No matter how hard you try to
freeze it, it will never return to its true shape.

Apologizing doesn't always mean you are
wrong. At times, you do it because you value
the relationship and love the person more than
your pride.

Once in a while in the middle of an ordinary
life, love gives us a fairytale.

Love sought is good but given unsought is better.

William Shakespeare

When I am with you my world is perfect.

People don't always need advice.
Sometimes all they need is a hand to hold,
an ear to listen and a heart to understand
them.

When someone loves you, they don't always
have to say it. You can always know it by the
way they treat you.

Carson Kolhof

"A woman's like a rose; if you treat her right, she'll bloom, if you don't, she'll wilt."

The most memorable people in your life will be the ones who loved you when you weren't lovable.

For faults are beauties in a lover's eyes.

Theocritus.

Forgiveness is the best form of love.

64

When I truly care for someone, their mistakes never change my feelings because it's the mind that gets angry while the heart still cares.

Hugs are pure medicine.

Find someone that isn't afraid to admit they miss you. Someone that knows you're not perfect but treats you as if you are.
Someone who couldn't imagine losing you.
Someone who gives their heart to you completely.
Someone who says, "I love you" and proves it.
Last but not least, find someone who wouldn't mind waking up with you in the morning, seeing your wrinkles and grey hair but still falls in love with you all over again.

You may fall in love with the beauty of
someone but remember that finally you have
to live with the character, not the beauty.

Missing someone is your hearts way of
reminding you that you love them.

A woman's beautiful face attracts a flirter.
A woman's beautiful heart attracts a lover.
A woman's beautiful character attracts a man.

A relationship without trust is like a car
without gas, you can stay in it all you want
but it won't go anywhere.

I can't promise you a perfect relationship
but what I can promise you is that if you're
trying, I'm staying.

My heart was taken by you, broken by you
and now it's in pieces because of you.

Every time we talk, I fall a little harder.

In a true relationship, your partner is also
your best friend.

"True marriage is based on happiness that comes from giving, serving, sharing, sacrificing and selflessness."

Spencer W. Kimball, LDS

I don't care about who was before me as long as I know there's nobody during me.

When you left, I lost a part of me.

Tears are how the heart speaks when our lips cannot describe how much we've been hurt.

Jealousy: It is the green-eyed monster that doth mock the meat it feeds on.

William Shakespeare

A good relationship is when someone accepts your past, supports your present and encourages your future.

Across the gateway of my heart
I wrote, "No Thoroughfare."
But love came laughing by and cried;
"I enter everywhere."

Herbert Shipman

Keep not your kisses for my dead cold brow.
The way is lonely, let me feel them now.

Some pray to marry the man they love.
My prayer will somewhat vary:
I humbly pray to heaven above,
That I love the man I marry.

All women want real love but their passion
for bargains leads them to accept cheap
imitations.

The anger of lovers renews the strength
of love.

A million words would not bring you back,
I know because I tried.
Neither would a million tears, I know because
I tried.

I wanted to be his life preserver, the thing
that would keep him afloat.
Instead, he became my anchor and I'm tired
of drowning.

Amanda Grace

She stood a sight to make an old man young.

It's hard to take a roll in someone's life when
you're not even part of the script.

My bounty is as boundless as the sea,
my love as deep.
The more I give to thee, the more I have
for both are infinite.

William Shakespeare

A man is already halfway in love with a
woman who listens to him.

I keep myself busy with things to do but
every time I pause, I still think of you.

Ever since time began, people have
recognized their true love by the light in
their eyes.

One word frees us of all weight and pain
of life, that word is love.

Sophocles

The human heart is a strange vessel.
Love and hatred can exist side by side.

Tears shed for another person are not a sign
of weakness. They are a sign of a pure heart.

An argument is always about what has been
made more important than the relationship.

Love in the heart is better than honey in
the mouth.

There is never a time or place for true love.
It happens accidentally, in a heartbeat,
in a single flashing, throbbing moment.

The day I met you, I was beside myself
with joy.

I would die for you but I won't live for you.

This is a good sign, having a broken heart.
It means we have tried for something.

Elizabeth Gilbert

A woman's heart should be so hidden in
God that a man has to seek him just to find
her.

Max Lucado

Love is an untamed force when we try to
control it, it destroys us.
When we try to imprison it, it enslaves us.
When we try to understand it,
it leaves us feeling lost and confused.

Paul Coelho

Maybe it's not always about trying to fix
something broken.
Maybe it's about starting over and creating
something better.

There's a difference between pretty and
beautiful.
When someone is pretty they have a good
appearance.
When someone is beautiful,
they shine on the inside and outside.

Flirtation is the froth on top of the wine of
love.

So Jacob worked seven years for Rachel
and they seemed like a few days because
he loved her.

Gen. 29:20

I want someone who says, "I love you"
every night and will prove it every day.

The ultimate test of a relationship is to
disagree but to hold hands.

I just want to be the girl you talk about.
The only one you couldn't live without.
To be the one who makes your heart beat
crazy and for you to say to your friends,
"she's my baby."

Always be a first-rate version of yourself
instead of a second-rate version of
someone else.

When the evening of this life comes,
we shall be judged on love.

St. John of the Cross

May I print a kiss on your lips I asked?
She nodded her sweet permission.
So we went to press and I rather guess,
We printed a large edition.

Love's sweetest meanings are unspoken;
the full heart known no rhetoric of words
and resorts to the pantomime of sighs and
glances.

There is no disguise that can for long conceal love where it exists or simulate it where it does not.

Love is to the moral nature exactly what the sun is to the earth.

Women are made to be loved not understood.

Married people should be best friends; no relationship on earth needs friendship as much as marriage.

Marion D. Hanks, LDS

Love not returned is like a question without an answer.

Those who love too much, hate in the same extreme.

Distance between two hearts is not an obstacle, rather a reminder of how strong love can be.

Why did I fall for you when you kept falling for her?

The first time I saw you, my heart whispered, that's the one.

Happily ever after is so once upon a time.

The falling out of lovers is the renewal
of love.

It takes a strong person to say they are
sorry and an even stronger person to forgive.

It's only after someone is gone do you
realize how much you love them.

True love will never fade unless it was a lie.

Loving you is my favorite mistake.

My heart bleeds no more since turning
to stone.

You can't buy love but you can pay
heavily for it.

The best and most beautiful things in this
world cannot be seen or even heard but
must be felt with the heart.

Love, when founded in the heart,
will show itself in a thousand
unpremeditated sally of fondness.

He gave her a look that you could
have poured on a waffle.

Don't you dare remember me when she
gets over you.

The lover's soul dwells in the body of
another.

True love is like a ghost, who everybody talks about and few have seen.

I would give up everything for one moment with you; for one moment is better than a lifetime of not knowing you.

Love may not ask you to give up your life but it will require lots of sacrifices.

Life without love is like a tree without blossom and fruit.

Khalil Gibran

So, there's this boy and the way he laughs
makes me smile, the way he talks gives me
butterflies.
Just everything about him makes me happy,
I love him.

If I know what love is, it's because of you.

Love is the master key that opens the gate
of happiness.

To get the full value of joy, you must have
someone to divide it with.

It's easy falling in love.
The hard part is finding someone to
catch you.

True love is when everything in the world
is going wrong and all you have to do is
look at that special person, then suddenly,
everything in the world is right again.

Love can sometimes be magic but magic
can sometimes be an illusion.

Javan

Together forever, never apart.
Maybe in distance but never in heart.

Within you I lose myself.
Without you I find myself wanting to
become lost again.

My favorite place to be is inside of your
hugs where it's warm and loving.

If I could be any part of you, I'd be your tears.
To be conceived in your heart, born in your
eyes, live on your cheeks and die on your lips.

My soul is moist if I don't have your sun
to dry it.

A kiss without a hug is like a flower without the fragrance.

There was a moon that evening but when you left, it hid behind a cloud humiliated.

Give me your hand and we will run together forever.

Love is like a dove, it's beautiful when it's there but it can fly away when you don't want it to.

I have written a love story without a
beginning or ending, so that we may
write it together.

Love talked about is easily turned aside
but love demonstrated is irresistible.

Our joy now and forever is inextricably
tied to our capacity to love.

John H. Groberg, LDS

Some people come into our lives and quickly
leave.
Some stay for a while leave footprints on our
hearts and then we are never ever the same.

Expectation is the root of all heartaches.

William Shakespeare

There's this place in me where your
fingerprints still rest, your kisses still linger
and your whispers softly echo.
It's the place where a part of you will
forever be a part of me.

Gretchen Kemp

Love is like the sun coming out of the
clouds and warms your soul.

What is the opposite of two?
A lonely me, a lonely you.

Your words are my food, your breath my
wine. You are everything to me.

Sarah Bernhardt

In the entire world, there is no heart for me
like yours.
In the entire world there is no love for you
like mine.

Maya Angelou

Kiss me and you may see stars.
Love me and I will give them to you.

Grow old along with me, the best is yet to be.

The best love is the kind that awakens the
soul and makes us reach for more.
The kind that plants a fire in our hearts and
brings peace to our minds and that's what
you've given me.

The Notebook

Sometimes your nearness takes my breath
away and all the things I want to say,
can find no voice.
Then in silence, I can only hope my eyes
will speak my heart.

My heart is ever at your service.

William Shakespeare

You give me the kind of feeling people
write about in novels.

Sarah Dessen

I'm wearing the smile you gave me.

It seems right now that all I've ever done
in my life is making my way here to you.

The Bridges of Madison County

I'll follow you and make a heaven out of hell
and I'll die by your hand which I love so well.

William Shakespeare

You're the one that I wanted to find.

With you my life is complete.

J. Wilson

Great love is when you shed tears yet still
care.
It's when you are ignored and you still
long for him.
It's when he begins to love another.
Yet you still smile and say, "I am happy
for you."

At the touch of love everyone becomes poet.

Plato

Love is a friendship set to music.

If I could have all the time in the world,
I know what I would do.
I'd spend the time in pleasure sublime,
Just by being with you.

No sooner met but they looked; no sooner
looked but they loved; no sooner loved but
they sighed; no sooner sighed but they
asked one another the reason;
no sooner knew the reason but they sought
the remedy.

If you love someone showing them is better
than telling them.
If you stop loving someone, telling them is
better than showing them.

A man falls in love through his eyes,
a woman through her ears.

I love her and that's the beginning of
everything.

Robert Frost

The hours I spend with you I look upon as
sort of a perfumed garden, a dim twilight
and a fountain singing to it.
You and you alone make me feel that I am
alive.
Other men it is said have seen angels but
I have seen thee and thou art enough.

Love is not what the mind thinks but what
the heart feels.

A loving marriage helps transform us from
the person we once were to the marvelous
person we were always meant to be.

Walking with your hand in mine and mine
in yours, that's exactly where I want to be
always.

I almost wish we were butterflies and lived but three summer days. Three such days with you I could fill with more delight than fifty common years could ever contain.

John Keats

Life is so short so fast the lone hours fly. We ought to be together, you and I.

To die and part is a less evil but to part and live, there is torment.

George Landsdowne

Romance is thinking about your significant other when you are supposed to be thinking about something else.

Nicholas Sparks

The most important things are the hardest
to say because words diminish them.
Somewhere there is someone that dreams
of your smile and finds in your presence
that life is worthwhile.
So, when you are lonely remember its true,
Someone somewhere is thinking of you.

Sometimes when one person is missing,
the whole world seems depopulated.

Lamartine

Never part without loving words to think
of during your absence.
It may be that you will not meet again in
this life.

Jean Paul Richter

My heart is yours my soul you have,
For your loss I would bitterly cry.
For I have been in love with you,
Since the moment you caught my eye.

I. Wilson

Love is the most beautiful thing to have,
hardest thing to earn and most painful
thing to lose.

When you need me, just whisper my name
in your heart. I will be there.

It's okay to lose your pride over someone you
love.
Don't lose someone you love over your pride.

Love that does not renew itself every day
becomes a habit and in turn slavery.

Sand and Foam

Love is not just affectionate feelings but
a steady wish for the loved person's
ultimate good as far as it can be obtained.

C.S. Lewis

The older I get; the less time I want to spend
with the part of the human race that didn't
marry me.

Marriage is a thousand little things that
make up the sum of our vows.

One sees clearly only with the heart.
Anything essential is invisible to the eyes.

Antoine de Saint Exupery

99

Marriage is a partnership of two unique people who bring out the very best in each other and who know that even though they are wonderful as individuals, they are even better together.

I've learned that no one is perfect until you fall in love with them.

This is the miracle that happens every time to those who really love; the more they give, the more they possess.

If you remember me, then I don't care if everyone else forgets.

Haruki Murakami

Sorrow is how we learn to love.
Your heart isn't breaking.
It hurts because it's getting larger.
The larger it gets, the more love it holds.

Rita Mae Brown

Having a partner in this lifetime to grow
together, love completely, ride out every
storm and overcome all of life's challenges
with, is one of the most beautiful blessings
of marriage.

There is in the heart of woman such a
deep well of love that no age can freeze it.

O, how this spring of love resembleth the
uncertain glory of an April day!

William Shakespeare

Life is the flower for which love is the honey.

I fell in love with her when we were together,
then fell deeper in love with her in the years
we were apart.

Nicholas Sparks

Love is the thing that enables a woman to sing
while she mops up the floor after her husband
has walked across it in his barn boots.

You could have had anything else in the
world and you asked for me.
She smiled up at him. Filthy as he was,
covered in blood and dirt, he was the most
beautiful thing she'd ever seen.
But I don't want anything else in the world.

Cassandra Clare

The best thing about me is you.

"It is a risk to love, what if it doesn't work out? Ah but what if it does!"

A house without love is not a home.

Love is a gross exaggeration of the difference between one person and everybody else.

Sometimes it's a form of love just to talk to somebody that you have nothing in common with and still be fascinated by their presence.

David Byrne

It is love that makes the impossible possible.

The one you love and the one who loves
you are never, ever the same person.

Chuck Palahniuk

The beauty that you have brought into
my life is beyond description.
I hardly can express it in words.
My heart speaks a new language now.

Emily Stimson

How delicious is the winning of a kiss
at love's beginning.

Thomas Campbell

Love lives on and hath a power to bless
when they who loved are hidden in the grave.

Love is the emblem of eternity; it confounds
all notion of time; removes all memory of a
beginning, all fear of an end.

Madame de Staël.

You never lose by loving.
You always lose by holding back.

Barbara De

If I know what love is, because of you.

Herman Hesse

I have found the paradox, that if you love
until it hurts, there can be no more hurt,
only more love.

Mother Teresa

Just the thought of being with you tomorrow
is enough to get me through the day.

Every heart sings a song incomplete until
another heart answers back.

I have learned not to worry about love,
but to honor its coming, with all my heart.

I miss you even more than I could have
believed and I was prepared to miss you
a good deal.

Love sacrifices all things to bless the thing
it loves.

Bulwer-Lytton.

Accept the things to which fate binds you
and love the people with whom fate brings
you together but do so with all your heart.

A good marriage is like a casserole,
only those responsible for it really know
what goes in it.

Love sees roses without thorns.

The beauty of marriage is not always seen from the very beginning but rather as love grows and develops over time.

Love is not blind; it sees but it doesn't mind.

Love can hope where reason would despair.

Pure love and suspicion cannot dwell together, at the door where the latter enters, the former makes its exit.

Alex. Dumas.

The first sigh of love is the last of wisdom.

Love is missing someone whenever
you're apart but somehow feeling
warm inside because you're close in heart.

Faith makes all things possible,
love makes all things easy.

Dwight L. Moody

A loving heart is the truest wisdom.

Charles Dicken

Who would give a law to lovers?
Love is unto itself a higher law.

Boethius

Do all things with love.

Og Mandino

I've got to let him go, so he can know,
just how much I love him.
Maybe if I'm lucky, he'll come back but
if not, I can make it through this.

The one thing we can never get enough
of is love and the one thing we never give
enough of is love.

We sat side by side in the morning light
and looked out at the future together.

I would have followed him to hell,
if he asked me and maybe I did.

Loving someone is like caring for a garden.
Love it too much or too little and it dies.
If you love it just right it will live forever.

It is difficult to know at what moment
love begins; it is less difficult to know
that it has begun.

Henry Wadsworth Longfellow

Love is life and if you miss love,
you miss life.

Leo Buscaglia

If you live to be 100, I hope to be 100 minus
1 day, so I never have to live without you.

I want a marriage more beautiful than my
wedding.

I believe in the compelling power of love.
I do not understand it; I believe it to be the
most fragrant blossom of all this thorny
existence.

Theodore Dreise

Elegance is the only beauty that never fades.

People who throw kisses are hopelessly lazy.

As soon go kindle fire with snow,
as seek to quench the fire of love with words.

William Shakespeare

No relationship is all sunshine but once
you've learned how to play in the rain,
you've discovered the secret to surviving
the passing storm together.

Being loved makes us smile.
Being married makes us grow and smile.

It's called flirting when you're in a
relationship and being friendly when
you're single.

Fortune and love favor the brave.

There is nothing more admirable than two
people who see eye to eye keeping house as
man and wife, confounding their enemies
and delighting their friends.

The hours I spend with you I look upon as
sort of a perfumed garden, a dim twilight and
a fountain singing to it. You and you alone
make me feel that I am alive.
Other men it is said, have seen angels but
I have seen thee and thou art enough.

Love is not what the mind thinks but what the heart feels.

A loving marriage helps transform us from the person we once were to the marvelous person we were always meant to be.

Walking with your hand in mine and mine in yours, that's exactly what I want, always.

Only choose in marriage a man whom you would choose as a friend if he were a woman.

Joseph Joubert

Family is where life begins and love never ends.

The most desired gift of love is not diamonds or roses or chocolate.
It's focused attention.

Love must be as much a light, as it is a flame

Love and respect will make any good relationship better.

A marriage is a gift. It should be opened up and enjoyed.

Where we love is home, home that our feet
may leave but not our hearts.

Oliver Wendell Holmes, Sr.

My philosophy: If it doesn't add love, trust
and value to your life, it doesn't belong in
your life.

If you want to know where your heart is,
look to where your mind goes when it
wonders.

When I am with you, the only place
I want to be is closer.

"Love is a promise; love is a souvenir, once given never forgotten, never let it disappear."

If ever you say, "you don't love me."
If ever you say, "you don't care."
If ever you say, "you don't want me,"
I will die that minute I swear.

We have the greatest pre-nuptial agreement in the world. It's called love.

Gene Perret

Keep choosing happiness and happiness will keep choosing you.

Of all forms of caution, caution in love is
perhaps the most fatal to true happiness.

We adore more than we irritate, that's why
we've lasted so long.

Cathy Thorne

Time to leave, how long can one
continue to nurse an ailing heart?
True love will come one day.

There is no such thing as a perfect man
or a perfect marriage.
The one I have is perfect for me.

Women hope men will change after marriage
but they don't; men hope women won't
change but they do.

Waiting for you is like waiting for rain in a
drought, useless and disappointing.

The most painful goodbyes are the ones
that are never explained.

Love can sometimes be magic.
But magic can sometimes be an illusion.

Marriage is like a fine wine, if tended
properly, it just gets better with age.

Coming together is a beginning.
Keeping together is progress.
Working together is success.

Marriage:
Love is the reason.
Lifelong friendship is the gift.
Kindness is the cause.
Till death do us part is the length.

A wise physician once said, "the best
medicine for humans is love."
Someone asked, "What if it doesn't work?"
He smiled and answered, "Increase the dose."

My husband is one of my greatest blessings
from God.
His love is a gift that I open every day.

Darlene Schacht

Love is when you meet someone who
tells you something new about yourself.

Bitterness imprisons life, love releases it.
Love is the beauty of the soul.

Saint Augustine

The people who hide their feelings usually
care the most.

You tell me, "You love me" but show me
you don't.

You may be out of my sight but never out
of my mind.

Keep love in your heart.
A life without it is like a sunless garden with
dead flowers.

Love me and my tears will stop.

Goodbyes will always hurt, pictures will
never replace being there, memories good
or bad will bring tears and words can never
replace feelings.

Part of me just wants to find the right words
to hurt you. The same way you hurt me.

I want to be the person you're scared to lose.

A house without love is not a home.

Love creates an "us" without destroying "me."

In love, somehow a man's heart is always either exceeding the speed limit or getting parked in the wrong place.

Love is sweet dream and marriage is the alarm clock.

Love is never without thorns.

Take each other for better or worse but not for granted.

Romance is the icing but love is the cake.

Fire in the heart sends smoke into the head.

Love is blind and marriage is a real eye opener.

Love does not cause suffering.
What causes it is the sense of ownership,
which is love's opposite.

Antoine de Saint Exupery

Words of love are works of love.

W. R. Alger.

Loved is proved by letting go.

The perfection of outward loveliness is the
soul shining through its crystalline covering.

Jane Porter

Till I loved, I never lived enough.

Emily Dickson

In men desire begets love and in women love begets desire.

Swift

What is love?

In math, an equation,
In history, a war,
In chemistry, a reaction,
In art, a heart,
In me, You.

The greatest pleasure of life is love.

The sun was brought to its knees when you entered this world, for now you are the brightest star to shine upon the earth.

127

My Dearest Friend

I- nspire Warmth

L-isten To Each Other
O-pen Your Heart
V-alue Your Union
E-xpress Your Trust

Y-ield To Good Sense
O-verlook Mistakes
U-nderstand Differences

Women are the poetry of the world in the same sense as the stars are the poetry of heaven. Clear, light-giving, harmonious, they are the terrestrial planets that rule the destinies of mankind.

Love can hope, where reason would despair. The greatest pleasure of life is love.

Sir W. Temple.

In men desire begets love and in women love begets desire.

Love needs no map, for it can find its way blindfolded.

Life is less than nothing without love.

Bailey

Don't use your eyes to look for love for it's your heart that knows it. Let yourself make mistakes and do learn from this. It is from this that you will accumulate your knowledge as to whether the person met is the one or not.

Never waste an opportunity to tell someone you love them.